Seasons

by Annabelle Lynch

W

FRANKLIN WATTS

LONDON•SYDNEY

Franklin Watts

First published in Great Britain in 2015 by The Watts Publishing Group

Copyright © 2015 The Watts Publishing Group

Series editor: Julia Bird
Series consultant: Catherine Glavina
Series designer: Peter Scoulding

Every attempt has been made to clear copyright. Should there be any inadvertent omission please apply to the publisher for rectification.

Picture acknowledgements: Jody Ann/Shutterstock: 8-9, 22tr. dean bertoncelj/Shutterstock: 20tl, 22cl. Creative Travel Projects/Shutterstock: 6-7, 22clb. Emi/Shutterstock: 18-19, 22bl. Irin-k/Shutterstock: front cover. Natalia K/Shutterstock: 21br. Kekyalyaynen/Shutterstock: 1, 21tr. Michael Kraus/Shutterstock: 21l. Lucy Liu/Shutterstock: 20tr. Mny-Jhee/Shutterstock: 14-15, 22tl. NataSnow/Shutterstock: 12-13, 22cr. Sergey Novikov/Shutterstock: 10-11. Richard Schramm/Shutterstock: 4-5. sumikophoto/Shutterstock: 16-17, 22br. Olena Zaskochenko/Shutterstock: 20b.

MIX
Paper from
responsible sources
FSC® C104740
FSC
www.fsc.org

HB ISBN: 978 1 4451 3859 6
PB ISBN: 978 1 4451 3861 9

Dewey number: 620.1

Printed in China

Franklin Watts
An imprint of
Hachette Children's Group
Part of The Watts Publishing Group
Carmelite House
50 Victoria Embankment
London EC4Y 0DZ

An Hachette UK Company
www.hachette.co.uk

www.franklinwatts.co.uk

Contents

What are seasons?

spring

summer

There are four seasons in a year. The weather is different in each season.

autumn

winter

Spring

In spring, the weather gets warmer after winter. New plants grow.

New life

Babies are often
born in spring.

Summer fun

In summer, the Sun shines. We have fun outside.

Time to **grow**

Plants and crops grow best in summer.

Autumn

In autumn, leaves change colour and fall to the ground.

Ready for **winter**

Some animals eat lots of food in autumn. Squirrels hide nuts to eat later.

Winter

Winter is cold.
Sometimes, it snows.
Plants and animals
wait for spring to
come again.

The right clothes!

We wear different
clothes when it is
sunny, rainy or cold.
When would you wear
these things?

Word bank

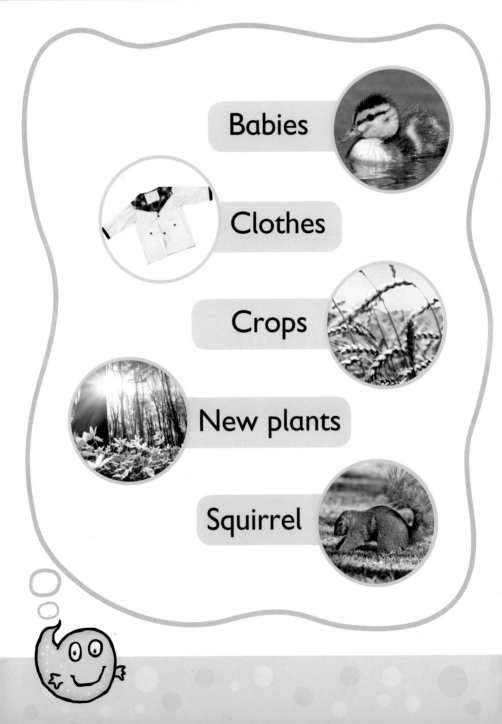

Babies

Clothes

Crops

New plants

Squirrel

Quiz

1. Babies are often born in

a) spring
b) summer
c) autumn.

2. Plants and crops grow best in

a) spring
b) summer
c) winter.

3. Some animals eat lots of food in

a) spring
b) summer
c) autumn.

Turn over for answers!

Notes for adults

TADPOLES are structured to provide support for newly independent readers. The books may also be used by adults for sharing with young children.

Starting to read alone can be daunting. **TADPOLES** help by providing visual support and repeating words and phrases. These books will both develop confidence and encourage reading and rereading for pleasure.

If you are reading this book with a child, here are a few suggestions:

1. Make reading fun! Choose a time to read when you and the child are relaxed and have time to share the book.
2. Talk about the content of the book before you start reading. Look at the front cover and blurb. What expectations are raised about the content? Why might the child enjoy it? What connections can the child make with their own experience of the world?
3. If a word is phonically decodable, encourage the child to use a 'phonics first' approach to tackling new words by sounding the words out.
4. Invite the child to talk about the content after reading, returning to favourite pages and pictures. Extend vocabulary by examining the Word Bank and by discussing new concepts.
5. Give praise! Remember that small mistakes need not always be corrected.

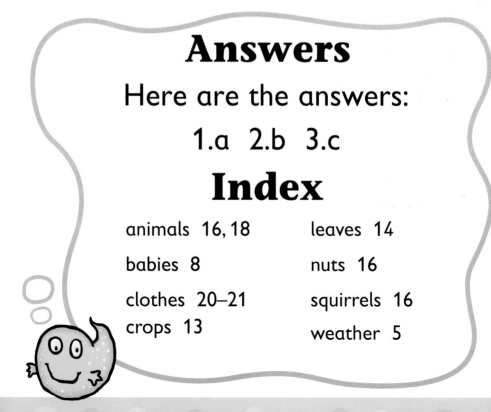

Answers

Here are the answers:

1.a 2.b 3.c

Index